THE FAERIES AND i

How I Discovered the Faeries

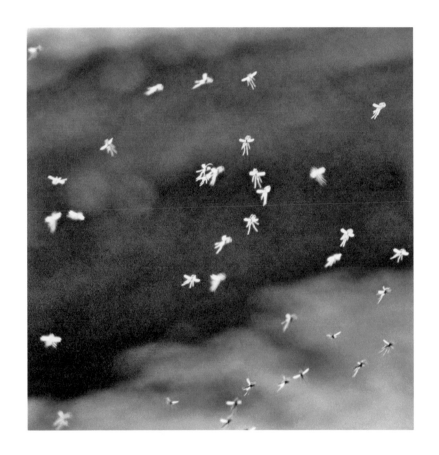

BY JAI HARVEY WRIGHT

AuthorHouse™
1663 Liberty Drive
Bloomington, IN 47403
www.authorhouse.com
Phone: 1 (833) 262-8899

Because of the dynamic nature of the Internet, any web addresses or links contained in this book may have changed
since publication and may no longer be valid. The views expressed in this work are solely those of the author and do
not necessarily reflect the views of the publisher, and the publisher hereby disclaims any responsibility for them.

Any people depicted in stock imagery provided by Getty Images are models,
and such images are being used for illustrative purposes only.
Certain stock imagery © Getty Images.

This book is printed on acid-free paper.

Interior Image Credit: Jai Harvey Wright

ISBN: 978-1-6655-0027-2 (sc)
ISBN: 978-1-6655-0026-5 (e)

Library of Congress Control Number: 2020918005

Print information available on the last page.

Published by AuthorHouse 09/30/2020

authorHOUSE®

THE FAERIES AND I

FINDING IDENTIFYING HOW AND WHERE THEY LIVE

DEDICATION

TO ASHLEY THE STRONGEST PERSON I KNOW. TO ALL MY GRANDCHILDREN, THE FAERIES
WILL ALWAYS BE A PART OF WHO YOU ARE EVEN WHEN YOU DON'T SEE IT
YOU MAKE ME A BETTER PERSON EVERY DAY.

ACKNOWLEDGMENTS

FOR BILL SINGLETON FOR HAULING THOSE LONG HIKES WHILE I FIND THE FAERIES AND
TO PHOTOGRAPH THEM. AND FOR THE FAERIES, SPRITES, PIXIES, HOBGOBLINS, GNOMES
ALL THE WEE FOLK I HAVE HAD THE HONOUR TO PHOTOGRAPH AND TO SPEND TIME
WITH YOU THANK YOU.

CONTENTS

I saw you from the ground you see

But never blinked an eye at me

I took a photo of the breeze

And yet you sat there in the trees

What do you think there in the tree

While you sit and ponder me

You sat so still and barely moved

But never blinked an eye at me

Because i saw you from the ground you see

I knew they were there… …It was just making them feel comfortable enough to let me take photos of them while they danced…...These little faeries since the first time I saw them have let me photograph them time and time again. I always thank them for their kindness. Not really sure if they appreciate my singing or not but I am happy to be around them.They are everywhere I go. In the morning I have my coffee and watch them dart around the flowers and the pond, sometimes so close I can almost touch them. Plant beautiful flowers for them and water stations in the yard to invite them in. Soon you will see them fluttering around your yard while watching them at a distance with great pleasure. Early in the morning or late at night you can see them. Do you see a soft flutter in the field that may be your first sprite soaring through the wheat field. If you are very patient they may stop to fly around you drawing your attention to them. Stop by the water and a light breeze passes you …..could be the little water sprites coming to meet you.

i froze i stopped, i didnt move,
you danced so soft among the breeze
The flowers swayed as tiny feet
Touched each petal sugar sweet

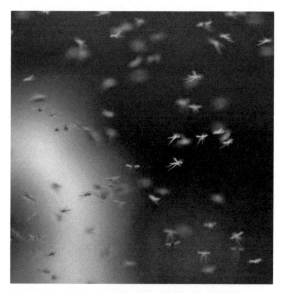

I have been truly blessed photographing the wee folk…..

I am of Irish descent and have always been raised around tales of faeries, banshees and such.

I spend a lot of time hiking, finding plenty of sightings of nature spirits in the woods, the gardens and the waters while out and about. These stories are mine, put together in this book for you to see the beauty that I find while enjoying the Wee Folk.

The photos and information put in this book are solely to help you find your own faeries, sprites, pixies, mushrooms, faery houses, wow the list is endless and to enjoy them for years to come.

Many times people walk in the woods or pathways of parks and completely overlook the Wee Folk. This book and its entirety will help you find them everywhere, you will get better and faster at finding many a Wee Folk. I will explain in small detail how I find the nature spirits, the faerie rings, the houses, all that is good and nature spirit worthy.

You've done the first step, you bought this book!

Learn the Signs of Faery Existence

I have taken a great many photos of faerie rings, faeries, sprites, toadstools, gnomes and the list is endless. I have been very fortunate on some of the wonderful sights I have seen

The more you learn about this wonderful faery world, the more you will want to learn and document it all.

Before you know it you will be finding all kinds of wonderful faery spots.

The thing is to walk slow. Keep your eyes open and begin a journey that I have taken many, many times.

Some of the wonderful little faeries and sprites dancing and playing around. It's truly a beautiful moment when you see them.

Faeries can be found all over in the oddest spots. Small mounds, tree stumps and gardens. It takes a special person to find faeries and once you learn how to spot a wee folk it gets easier. You will begin to see them everywhere and the excitement that ensues can overwhelm you. I still get excited seeing new faeries as I did the first day. Faeries can be found in the wilds or in your own backyard garden. They have been removed from their natural habitats very much like the wild creatures of the forest have been moved for housing and industry. To encourage faeries to spend time around your property, plant flowers and have water features, bird baths are good. Faeries like a beautiful well kept yard. Lavenders, blue bells, violets, coneflowers, rosemary and thyme are good for faery gardens. Faeries like small shiny things.But as always never iron things. Welcome the bugs, birds and bees. Faeries respond to how you treat the wildlife in your yard. Tell the faeries they are welcome in your yard.

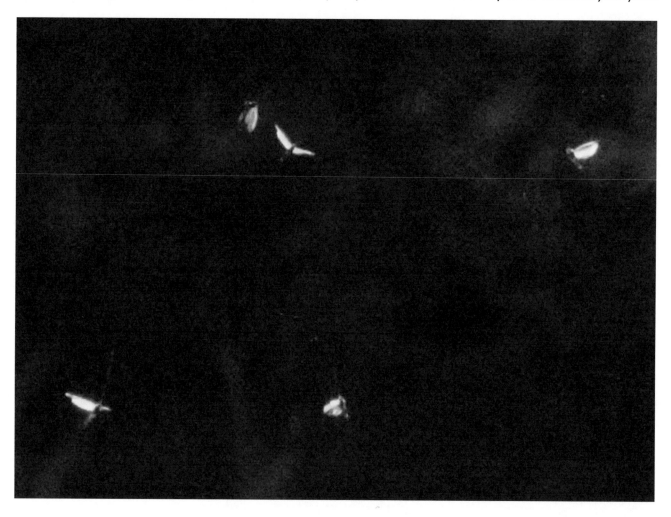

The Benefits of Faeries

Faeries make you feel like skipping or laughing. They bring out your inner child.

When you are walking in the woods or fields and you suddenly smell flowers…. That usually means faeries are nearby

You will greatly notice some changes in your being

Faeries make you happy, giddy and feel compassion.

Children are often able to see and hear faeries, because they haven't hardened their hearts on life and what it has to offer.

The Nature spirits can often change their appearance

You may suddenly see a bunny or a fox while out walking, does it make you feel happy and calm to see it….That may have been a faery. What about the butterfly following you around or the very strange things you see for a fleeting moment….all part of the faery realm. The more you discover this wonderful world of faeries the more you will understand the beauty therein.

But don't ever take advantage of them. Always be kind and happy for them, they will in return show you many wondrous adventures.

You could just imagine the faeries tugging on the tree
Come dance with me they said
Round and round we go
Come dance with me… ….

Sometimes they pause….
I wish i could see their eyes
Because when they pause….
It's my eyes they see….

Sprite.... a nimble elf like creature with clear see through wings, especially one associated with water. They are typically not a mean or difficult faery, unless you scare or startle them. Sprites can be found mostly around small lakes or streams, or even ponds and for the most part are very, very tiny. Also less powerful than a faery. Often being thought of as a small flying bug, lighting up the night as they travel around the ponds. They can breathe in water and air. You could find yourself in the presence of a sprite so try leaving them small dishes of water in a pretty dish not iron or steel. I like to grow white flowers around my pond to encourage the sprites. Sprites are the gardeners of the flowers. They will keep the pesky bugs from destroying the natural flowers. White creates bright and sprites do like light especially at night and in the wee hours of the morning.

They enjoy living in the woods, high in the trees, by water if possible. If you spot a sprite then consider that area a high traffic spot for nature spirits (sprites, pixies, faeries).Sprites will often take a bath in the dew of a flower. Ground or water sprites will bath in ponds and rivers..

I found the sprites by the wildflowers early in the evening

They were darting everywhere

The hobgoblin, what can I say I have photographed one before who was actually in the garden. I say that because they are usually found in the house doing odd chores in the wee hours. Waking up at night and can't figure why... maybe you have a hobgoblin and a not so quiet one. They will typically do odd jobs about the house and expect nothing but a morsel of food in payment. But don't ever pay them with new clothes or they will leave as quickly as they came, not wanting to clean your house or dust in new clothes.....no sir. Usually found wearing brown raggy clothing or nothing at all. A prankster at heart, they will move things and trick you sometimes but as long as you are happy with your hobgoblin let them be and accept their quirks. The hobgoblin will keep you on your toes. You will notice things mixed up your glasses will be in the cereal cupboard, the pop will be in the potato bin. That is when you know you have a hobgoblin. Try not to be upset with him but encourage him to hang out around your house. With any luck his whole family will move in. At first things may seem hectic but having a hobgoblin around your house will always be exciting. He will always have you scratching your head saying who put that there… …..

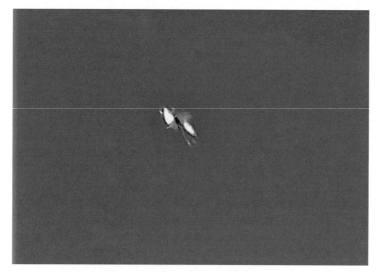

My little hobgoblin…..Hobgoblins are tiny mischievous little elves. They will always help around the house, the farm. When you know you have one start watching so you can photograph them.

Some faeries dancing on a hot summer night

Gnomes are to me some of the most wonderful little people around. If you decide to look you can find them almost anywhere you go…..or I should say they will find you . If a gnome shows themselves to you, it means you are very special and they are comfortable with you. I had such an experience many years ago. While the gnome let me take his picture and it wasn't until later that I looked at the photos , taken during the day I noticed the gentleman gnome in the photo. There he was warming himself by the fire clear as day. So there I sat at 2 in the a.m. looking for the first time at the gnome on the screen of my laptop, not really sure what I was looking at. As i began to read and study about gnomes I realized just how lucky I am that he showed himself to me in such a way. Gnomes are naturally homely creatures but that doesn't make them mean or scary. Homely is beautiful when talking about them. Gnomes that show themselves to people have become interested in the person and want to become a part of your life, protecting your property. They will cause havoc in your life when they get bored but they won't allow anyone to hurt what is theirs. The earth gnome was photographed on Saturday, May 16th 2015 in Woodville Ontario. He is wearing a blue coat with a red belt tied around his waist, and red pants. My gnome is a gentleman gnome and I was never sure of the age for they can live a very long time. I learned one thing about gnomes that they always have some seaweed in their pocket, a sparkle stone for lighting fires and a rabbit paw to heal. Then to that you add the cat's whisker to tease you and a small piece of soap to bathe.

He was cold and came to me by the fire. I was truly blessed to see him…..

When you come upon a faery house in the woods

The first thing you want to do is introduce yourself to the faeries. I have always done this especially with young children. You would want them to be introduced in a proper way. First thing you do is to let them know some things about you. Knock on the door small as it is and let the faery know who you are and why you are there.

Be respectful of the ground around the small home so as not to destroy the faery yard. A faery house and the ground around it are sacred space. If you have ever been visiting a faery house and smelled flowers for no reason …...usually means there is a faery close by. If you come to a pond and find a faery house use a bell to call upon the faeries. Tinkle the bell and within minutes you should see little ripples on the water or bubbles. Let faeries know you want to see them and visit with them. Faeries are very much interested in friendly light hearted people. Their houses come in many shapes and sizes and hundreds of styles. I have had the pleasure of photographing so many beautiful ones. Truly stunning houses and you can tell how much they love their little houses. Some are beautifully decorated with moss, mushrooms, twigs, leaves and even tiny flowers. Faeries love copper but are not fond of iron at all so never use iron around your faery spot. And always respect the faeries and they will stay for years.

A pathway to the faery house

FAERY TREES

These to me are two prime examples of FAERY TREES unique on their own for sure but as you can see in the top one the actual doors. The tree in the bottom picture has odd shaped doors. The roots actually help create the doors on the base of many faery trees. When you come upon a faery tree you must always knock on the door and introduce yourself. Tell the faery's something about who you are and always tell them to have a good day, (thus they in turn would wish the rest of the day to you, passing on the good luck).

If you see what looks like a door in the tree it probably is. Wee folk come in all shapes and sizes. Don't hesitate to knock on the door of a faery you will never know who may come to the door to greet you.
I am me and you are you
I've come to visit here I am
My name is me and you are you
Faery drink I want to taste
What you share I will feel graced
Good morning Faery how are you
I am me and you are you

Unique trees are almost always faery trees there is never a doubt.

Trees i climb, Trees i see, Trees for Faeries, Trees for Me

This was one of my first Faery Trees. I had one granddaughter knock on the door to say hello to the Faeries.

Please come knocking at my door
Come from land or come from shore
You are welcomed through my door
Sit a spell and rest your feet
Tell your stories of what you've seen
Of Faery tales and Faery Queen

This would be the type of tree the wee Faeries would really enjoy

If you look careful you can see the small pixie dust particles falling from the flower as the bee bops around it .

Here are water sprites flying around a small peaceful creek.

A small faery door at the base of a tree.

I found the ring and decided not to enter it
But instead gazed upon it wondering what group of faeries
Danced around it singing with happiness
Faery rings are typically made out of mushrooms and rocks
They usually occur naturally. The nature folk love to dance and sing around them
"Tethered" faery rings occur in a forest
The tree appears to have a rope tethered to and around it
I was lucky to take a picture of that. I like to think a faery ring is caused by the magic left behind when the faeries have danced the night away. It is said that you shouldn't disrupt the faerie ring. Take note of where you find the rings how big they are and what they are made of.

This particular faery ring caught me off guard in the middle of a field but I could certainly imagine the faeries dancing around it under the moon. I have through my photos found that certain roots of trees and flowers can produce the same type of faerie rings. They can be found all over the world in every country and are highly unexplainable. It's always been said that you must not at any time enter a Faery Ring for any reason. The theory behind the Faery Ring is that having entered it you would be transported to the Faery World never to return. But if curiosity gets the better of you try running around the Faery Ring during a full moon nine times, but only nine times no more no less. This allows you to go inside safely. You could also try entering the ring with your hat on backwards as to confuse the Faeries but why..... The wee folk love to be happy and to help your land and family flourish to be cruel in any way would just be wrong..... Faeries can be seen dancing around them in the wee hours of the night, I have yet to photograph this phenomena. The faeries live beneath the ring and any crops or farms nearby would surely flourish.

**THESE ARE SOME VERY GOOD EXAMPLES OF
TETHERED FAERY RINGS.**

*The faeries will flutter and flash their wings as they dance around the faery ring.
I would imagine it would be a truly beautiful sight.*

Rocks….. Houses are made with them, fences built, poems written, they are tossed in the air….. I could go on about rocks, but the most important is grounding. They can bring you peace, just sitting in a pile of rocks for some people is calming. After collecting a large assortment over the years I have learned one thing, rocks are beautiful and heavy lol. One of my favorites is a HAG STONE. My favorite spot to find them are the beaches. When you walk along the beach keep an eye on the rocks in and out of the water. What you're looking for is a rock with a hole all the way through it. A HAG STONE is lucky if you find it or acquire it on your own. Also called witch stones, serpent eggs and snake eggs. They are considered a protection amulet. They can be used to ward off the dead, curses, sickness and nightmares. It is said that you can put your worries through the hole and they will stay there.

HAGSTONE

Hang a hagstone on a red string, thread for good luck
They also regenerate your energy. They refresh your body, mind, and spirit with healing energy when a stone is hung over your bed at night.
Did I mention that hag stones were used as protection against the evil eye? Bad dreams, for good luck etc. bottom line is that if you can get your hands on a hag stone, treasure it and treat it like the sacred object that it is.
A hagstone knot, a cord containing several hagstones, hangs in the Natural History Museum in London and was believed to have been made in the 1800's.
There are some practitioners of Italian folk magic who also believe that fairy stones can be used to see and ultimately bind a faery to their service for a specific length of time; a dangerous practice for sure. If you have a hag stone or faery stone, wear it around your neck when you're out in nature looking for faeries. To "fine tune" your faery attraction skills, gather morning dew in a container and gently pour it through the hole in your fairy stone.

Peacock ore and the Faeries

Faeries enjoy happy colored things. Rock, gemstones, fossils all of them once we begin to connect with them they begin to turn our negative energy into positive. Peacock ore is just the right stone to do this. You become happy just holding a piece of Peacock ore.You will gain confidence in yourself carrying a piece of this iridescent stone. I hope the Faeries touch the stone for luck. Having written all of this lets you see one of the reasons why having a faery in your yard is so important. When you invite faeries into your yard, home or wherever you set aside a spot for them and begin to leave things for them aka peacock ore you invite a happy faery. The first time you actually see a faery you will be on a happy high. It may take some time for you to actually find signs a faery is around you but be patient you will find one.

Rock, gemstones, fossils all of them once we begin to connect with them they begin to turn our negative energy into positive. Bornite or peacock ore is one of these. (multicolored copper iron sulfide mineral ore) It's called the stone of happiness.This is probably why the wee folk love it so much. You don't very often hear of sad faeries. The ore encourages us to be more at peace and to align our perceptive abilities, allowing us to be calm and happy in all situations. If you have blocked energies this will help you to restore to your natural self.

OMAROLLUK FAERY HOLEY STONES A DOORWAY TO FAERIES

These rocks are made from sediment that gets trapped in it and over time wind and rain and water causes the sediment to pop out leaving a small round odd shaped indent in the rock. In some cases it leaves many indents in one rock. These particular ones were formed in the Belcher Islands of southeast Hudson Bay.They were carried southwest into central Canada by glaciers. The stones are said to be very lucky. Put one in your bedroom to bring on happy dreams about faeries. I go to beaches to find mine. Usually you can find a lot of them just walking along the beach. Every omarolluk is completely different from the next. I believe they have calming and healing effect when you handle them or have them around you. I always love rocks. Just sitting in a pile of rocks has been calming for me. An omarolluk hung with a red string by your bed (much like a hag stone) can prevent nightmares, and give you a better night's sleep. Carry one around in your pocket for luck and happiness. I could imagine the faeries sitting in the small holes taking baths on a hot summer night or swimming to keep cool. I believe rocks and the wee folk go hand and hand.

Ravens, what stunning creatures.

The first time I saw a raven I fell in love. They are truly some of the most beautiful birds I have ever seen. Then I found out they are part of the faery world. Imagine how happy I was. Ravens are shapeshifters. I believe they help protect the faeries. They are said to be able to change into human form. Further to that I think they can walk among the faeries by dwarfing themselves. When you see Ravens, know that faeries are close by. Ravens can imitate human and animal sounds. Sooooooo think you hear something in the woods…. I just think they are some of the most fascinating parts of the Faery Realm. Ravens are sensitive and will have sympathy for another raven that is suffering. Perhaps it's this empathy the Raven's have that the faeries understand.

The first is a picture of a Raven talking to me and then I captured a picture of what I thought was a fallen Raven. He was actually resting on the post. By hooking his feet into the side and pushing his beak into the top he could sleep on the post without falling off.

Never ingest any mushrooms found in the outdoors. When I think of mushrooms and toadstools alike, faeries come to mind.To me there has been a connection since time began.What I like to look for when photographing faery mushrooms is color and uniqeness. Amanita Muscaria is a red mushroom with pale spots on it. The faes and gnomes love to perch on top of this one. It contains two toxins that are extremely poison to people. In faeries though, it reduces the body's response to fear. Making it easy for them to protect their home from predators.

I don't very often find this type. I was pretty excited too!

Another example of a beautiful mushroom. You could just imagine the wonderful speeches the sprites and faeries would give while perched upon the top...

It's home, it's safe, it's where I sit. I ponder what you think of it. It's pretty, it's poisonous, it's complicated growth. I love to sit upon the lid,and stretch the stories far and wide of Faery Tales and Faery Pride.

Faery Moons happen only once every two or three years. It occurs when you have a second moon in one month. If you make a Faery Circle there is a good chance you will call the Faeries to you. I have had the chance over the years to photograph some beautiful Faery Moons.

Waiting by day for the Faery Moon
My name is Moon or so they say
I wait and wait til break of day
To see you Faery
By the Faery Moon

Every time there is a full Moon I think of the mystical world of Faeries

I believe they start to waken as the moon starts to rise. When the Moon is Full and the Faeries fly, that's when the real magic starts. Oh the nightly celebrations they must have. I guess it would depend upon what time of year it is what they are celebrating. During the Summer Solstice the layer between the Faery World and ours is quite thin.

If you have roses in your yard, probably the Faeries have found them. The smell is intoxicating to the Wee Folk. Leave shiny things in your garden for the Faeries. Nothing iron though. Iron makes Faeries very sick.

I leave little tiny bottles of colored glass and crystals around my yard. Flowers and more Flowers.

White flowers in your garden will bring Faeries in the evening. You will see lots of little Faeries flying around the garden at night.

Also leave little bowls of water around your yard. The more you try to make your yard a happy place for nature and Faeries it will happen....Faeries will come to the yard. The thing about Faeries is the more you look for them the more they will come looking for you. I think Faeries are very curious about people. Make your home a happy place and they will come to you

So this is the first book about THE FAERIES AND I. The beautiful wonderful wee folk that dance around the moon, your gardens, ponds, wheat fields....I could just go on and on. I hope you enjoy looking for the Faeries. You will get hooked on them and like me, you will begin to understand the special FAERY WORLD. Thank you for enjoying the book.

Here are a few of the Faeries from my yard

Solitary Faery

Printed in the United States
By Bookmasters